PEOPLE AT
THE CENTER OF

THE
CIVIL RIGHTS
MOVEMENT

By TAMRA B. ORR

BLACKBIRCH™
PRESS

GALE

San Diego • Detroit • New York • San Francisco • Cleveland
New Haven, Conn. • Waterville, Maine • London • Munich

THOMSON

GALE

LIBRARY OF CONGRESS CATALOGING-IN-PUBLICATION DATA

Orr, Tamra.
  The civil rights movement / by Tamra B. Orr.
    p. cm. — (People at the center of:)
Summary: Profiles people who led the civil rights movement in the United States, including Rosa Parks, Asa Philip Randolph, Ida B. Wells-Barnett, and Booker T. Washington.
Includes bibliographical references and index.
  ISBN 1-56711-763-5 (alk. paper)
  1. African American civil rights workers—Biography—Juvenile literature. 2. Civil rights workers—United States—Biography—Juvenile literature. 3. African Americans—Civil rights—History—Juvenile literature. 4. Civil right movements—United States—History—Juvenile literature. [1. Civil rights workers. 2. Political activists. 3. African Americans—Civil rights—History—20th century. 4. Civil rights movements—History—20th century. 5. Race relations. 6. African Americans—Biography.] I. Title. II. Series.

  E185.96.O77 2004
  323'.092'396073--dc21

                                                    2003005143

⊚ CONTENTS

PEOPLE AT THE CENTER OF

THE CIVIL RIGHTS MOVEMENT

Civil rights are a broad range of privileges and laws that guarantee freedoms, such as the right of free expression; the right to enter into contracts, own property, and initiate lawsuits; and the freedom to use public facilities. For decades in the United States, racial discrimination deprived many African Americans of these rights. Their efforts to end this discrimination were at the core of the Civil Rights movement.

Although the movement began in the United States in the 1950s, its roots can be traced back to events that followed the Civil War. During the war, President Abraham Lincoln's historical Emancipation Proclamation freed most slaves. The Thirteenth Amendment to the Constitution, which abolished slavery throughout the country, was passed three years later, in 1865. Most newly freed slaves had no money or property and were illiterate. Southern governments, bitter over the loss of the war enacted state laws called Black Codes that prevented African Americans from owning land and restricted their employment opportunities.

To try to improve the situation of black Americans, Congress approved the Civil Rights Act of 1866, which granted all blacks citizenship and forbade states from passing discriminatory laws. Next, Congress approved the Fourteenth Amendment, which guaranteed African Americans citizenship and granted them full and equal protection under the law. In 1870, the Fifteenth Amendment gave African American males the right to vote.

The 1870 passage of the Fifteenth Amendment allowed African American men to vote for the first time.

As blacks gained more rights, resentful southerners formed groups like the Ku Klux Klan, which terrorized and killed blacks and their white sympathizers. Congress again made an effort to help African Americans. It passed the Civil Rights Act of 1875, which gave all people the right to use any public building or place.

In 1883, a series of Supreme Court cases determined that a provision of the 1875 act was unconstitutional, and that owners and operators of public places were free to discriminate. Another setback for black Americans came two decades later after a young man named Homer Plessy refused to leave a seat on a railroad car reserved

Angered that blacks were gaining more rights, some southerners formed the Ku Klux Klan and similar groups to terrorize blacks and prevent them from exercising their newly won rights.

As a result of the 1896 Supreme Court ruling in Plessy v. Ferguson, *African American students in the South could only attend "separate but equal" schools, like the one pictured above.*

for whites and was arrested. Determined to challenge the law, he sued the railroad company. His case, *Plessy v. Ferguson* (1896), went to the U.S. Supreme Court. Because Plessy was not denied access to a public place, the Court upheld the law that required "separate but equal" accommodations for whites and blacks. Soon after the landmark decision, southern states adopted a wave of legislation—known as Jim Crow laws—that segregated facilities in public places.

Although blacks were theoretically equal to whites under the law, the Jim Crow laws meant that they were kept separate from whites and treated like second-class citizens. The situation for black Americans only worsened. In some sections of the South, blacks were beaten for the slightest infraction, real or imagined. Toward the end of the nineteenth century, lynchings (hanging by a mob) became epidemic, and thousands of blacks were killed.

The federal government took little action to enforce civil rights for blacks after 1900, and individual states continued to enact discriminatory legislation. As a result, by the middle of the twentieth century, blacks in the South still found themselves segregated from whites in schools and other public places. Even though they legally had the right to vote, in reality many were kept from voting by obstacles such as poll taxes that they could not afford and literacy tests they could not pass.

To abolish these segregationist laws, and to increase educational opportunities for black children, the National Association for the Advancement of Colored People (NAACP) was founded in 1909. In the 1950s a group of lawyers from the NAACP argued before the Supreme Court that segregation of black children in the public schools was unconstitutional because it violated the Fourteenth Amendment. The Court agreed. Its landmark decision *Brown v. Board of Education of Topeka, Kansas,* (1954) determined that the doctrine of "separate but equal" was unconstitutional in public education and overturned the *Plessy v. Ferguson* ruling. For the first time, blacks and whites were enrolled in schools together in an action called integration.

The change was not easy or welcome, and blacks were often met with violent resistance to the law.

The focus of the *Brown* decision was on the desegregation of public schools. The next big hurdle for the movement involved the desegregation of public transportation. In 1955, a black woman named Rosa Parks was arrested in Montgomery, Alabama, for refusing to give up her seat to a white passenger on a bus. Her act led to nonviolent protest in the form of a

In 1954, when the U.S. Supreme Court ruled that the segregation of public schools was illegal, some whites resisted integration with violence.

boycott that lasted more than a year, and a Supreme Court ruling in 1956 that the Montgomery segregation laws were unconstitutional. Empowered by the boycott's success, the Southern Christian Leadership Conference (SCLC) formed to support the civil rights struggle, and the tactics of nonviolent protest dominated the movement.

In many southern states, custom—consistent with local and state laws—prevented blacks and whites from sitting together in public places such as lunch counters. In 1960, four black college students determined to challenge segregation entered a

Woolworth's department store in Greensboro, North Carolina, and ordered coffee at an all-white lunch counter. Although denied service, they refused to leave. By the tenth day of their protest, people in five states were following their example and holding their own sit-ins. Months later the newly formed Student Nonviolent Coordinating Committee (SNCC), an outgrowth of the SCLC, helped organize sit-ins and other protests against segregated establishments. Over the next two years, in cities throughout the South, more than seventy thousand people, blacks and whites, used sit-ins to nonviolently protest segregation in places such as public swimming pools and libraries. These protesters frequently met with violence, but their actions resulted in the easing of segregation laws in some states.

Although Supreme Court rulings banned segregation, federal and state officials rarely enforced the rulings, and African Americans still found themselves limited to separate waiting areas and railroad cars when traveling. In 1961, groups of people called Freedom Riders rode buses throughout the South to test the Supreme Court's

When these four black students refused to leave an all-white lunch counter in North Carolina in 1960, sit-ins became a new way to protest segregation.

1947 ruling that prohibited segregation on interstate buses and the 1960 ruling that banned segregation in bus terminals that served interstate routes. Many of the Freedom Riders were brutally attacked on their journeys, but they exposed the widespread blatant disregard for the Court's rulings. More importantly, their actions prompted legislation that forced bus companies to obey the ban on segregated terminals and railroad stations.

Similar protests continued until the early 1960s. In 1963, approximately 250,000 people marched on Washington in support of a sweeping new civil rights bill. The results of the march and of years of nonviolent protest culminated in the landmark legislation, the Civil Rights Act of 1964, which banned segregation in public places and racial discrimination in employment and education.

In 1965, Congress passed the Voting Rights Act, which eliminated previous voting barriers and provided for federal action and enforcement to remove those obstacles. As a result, African Americans voted in record numbers, especially in Mississippi, where registered black voters rose from 6.7 percent to almost 60 percent in 1967.

Despite growing support for the civil rights cause, many young African Americans, often those who lived in poverty,

Riots destroyed poorer areas of major cities in the late 1960s. By that time, many younger African Americans had grown tired of the slow progress toward racial equality and turned to violence.

believed progress came too slowly and the continuing violence against blacks could no longer be tolerated. These black Americans began to turn to leaders who advocated self-defense through violence. Between 1964 and 1969, there were hundreds of riots, primarily in larger cities. The concepts of Black Pride and Black Power emerged, and the movement began to split into different factions. By the late 1960s, black separatists lost support as blacks and whites alike grew weary of the fighting and destruction of communities.

Despite the splintering in the movement, however, the positive gains achieved by the dedication of those who fought for civil rights were substantial. As a result of the movement, Africans Americans won the right to shop, dine, or travel without fear; to vote freely; to hold elective offices; and to improve their economic status.

William Lloyd Garrison was born in 1805 in Massachusetts. Before he was twenty years old, he was well known as the author of many antislavery articles. In 1829, he traveled to Baltimore to edit and write for the *Genius of Universal Emancipation,* an antislavery journal.

In early 1831, Garrison produced the first issue of the *Liberator,* a small newspaper that he published for thirty-five years. It never had a large circulation, but its powerful antislavery messages influenced many people. That same year, Garrison helped organize the New England Anti-Slavery Society, and a few years later the American Anti-Slavery Society, two of the first organizations dedicated to the emancipation of slaves.

Garrison's goal was to speak out against slavery rather than establish a plan to end it. He felt that working to change the moral principles of his opponents was the best way to end slavery. He was never deterred in his belief that slavery should end immediately, an unpopular view in the 1830s. Although he spoke against the use of violence to achieve reform, his views often upset people. He received threatening letters and in 1835 was attacked by a mob in Boston.

After the ratification of the Thirteenth Amendment, Garrison prepared an editorial to be published in the last issue of the *Liberator* in December 1865. Three years later, his supporters presented him with thirty thousand dollars in appreciation for his dedication to the cause. He died in 1879 in New York.

LADIES' DEPARTMENT.

'Am I not a Woman and a Sister?'

White Lady, happy, proud and free,
Lend awhile thine ear to me ;
Let the Negro Mother's wail
Turn thy pale cheek still more pale.
Can the Negro Mother joy
Over this her captive boy,
Which in bondage and in tears,
For a life of wo she rears ?
Though she bears a Mother's name,
A Mother's rights she may not claim ;
For the white man's will can part,
Her darling from her bursting heart.

From the Genius of Universal Emancipation
LETTERS ON SLAVERY.—No. III.

Opposite: William Lloyd Garrison was one of the first Americans behind the movement to abolish slavery.
Above: Garrison printed this poem in the Liberator, *the antislavery newspaper he published from 1831 to 1865.*

FREDERICK DOUGLASS

FORMER SLAVE WHO FOUGHT FOR ABOLITION

Frederick Douglass was born into slavery in Maryland in 1817. When he was eight years old, his master's wife taught him how to read—even though it was illegal to educate slaves. When this instruction ended, Frederick, determined to continue his education, traded his food for reading lessons from neighborhood boys.

When Douglass was twenty, he escaped to the North by train with the assistance of a free black woman named Anna Murray. Once he reached New York City, he and Murray married. They later moved to Massachusetts. Within three years, Douglass was a lecturer for the Massachusetts Anti-Slavery Society and spoke throughout New England about his experiences as a slave. He spread the word about the growing anti-slavery movement and advocated racial equality.

Above: Frederick Douglass published three autobiographies that helped convince people that slavery was wrong. Opposite: A former slave who escaped to freedom, Douglass became a respected abolitionist and a powerful writer and orator.

In 1845, Douglass published *Narrative of the Life of Frederick Douglass, An American Slave*. It was an instant success and the first of three autobiographies. Douglass's ability to provide an accurate portrayal of the harsh realities of slavery through his writings convinced many people that slavery was wrong. His success was not all positive, however. His book included specific names, places, and other identifying details, and he began to live in fear of being taken back into captivity. To be safe, he sailed to England.

Douglass returned to New York in 1847 and founded a newspaper called the *North Star*. During the Civil War, he worked to recruit men to fight for the Union army. From 1889 to 1891, Douglass served as U.S. minister to Haiti. In the last few years of his life, Douglass spoke out against poll taxes and other attempts in the South to deny African Americans the vote. He died in 1895.

BOOKER T. WASHINGTON

FOUNDED THE TUSKEGEE INSTITUTE

Booker Taliaferro Washington was born into slavery in 1856, on a small tobacco plantation in Virginia. When Booker was nine years old, the Civil War ended, and he and his mother moved to West Virginia. He went to work in a salt furnace every morning at 4 A.M. and attended school afterward. At night, he taught himself to read. At sixteen, he enrolled at the Hampton Institute of Virginia, one of the first schools to accept African American students. There he developed his ideas of the right of a black man to an education and the concepts of self-reliance.

Washington believed that the key to success for any black person was to learn a useful or helpful service or skill. In 1881, he founded the Tuskegee Institute in Alabama to fulfill that mission. The school began in a run-down shack. He and his students built classrooms, dormitories, and a chapel and planted crops for food. By 1900, Tuskegee had forty buildings, and enrollment was up to four hundred students. Consistent with his philosophy, Washington focused on teaching vocational subjects and the virtues of hard work, rather than traditional academics.

In 1892, he established the annual Tuskegee Negro Conference, where thousands of blacks were taught efficient farming methods. In 1900 he created the National Negro Business League to support businesses owned and operated by blacks. His autobiography, *Up from Slavery*, became a best seller and

Opposite: Although Booker T. Washington was criticized for not taking a strong stand against racism, he was one of the most influential blacks of his time. Above: In 1881, Washington founded the Tuskegee Institute because he believed that education is the key to success.

later a classic among works about the rise of great men. Although Washington was well respected in business and political circles, many black leaders felt that his philosophies encouraged blacks not to fight for civil rights and ultimately only contributed to their worsening conditions. Washington died in 1915 at the age of fifty-nine.

IDA B. WELLS-BARNETT

Ida B. Wells was born to enslaved parents in Mississippi in 1862. Her parents died when she was a teenager, and she was left in charge of her five younger siblings. To support them, she took a job as a teacher. The family later moved to Memphis, Tennessee.

When Wells was twenty-six years old, she refused to give up her seat to a white man on a train car. Although the 1875 Civil Rights Act stated that discrimination was not allowed on transportation, many of the railroads ignored it. After Wells was forced off the train, she hired an attorney, sued the railroad, and won. When the railroad appealed to the Supreme Court of Tennessee, however, the lower court's ruling was reversed.

Under the pen name Iola, Wells wrote several newspaper articles about her experiences. She became a journalist and part owner of a Memphis newspaper, the *Memphis Free Speech*. When local whites murdered a black grocer and friend of Wells, she was outraged and wrote a series of fiery articles. In them, she accused white people of lynching black business owners to eliminate them as economic competition.

When she was away in New York, people in Memphis who were incensed by her articles destroyed the offices of *Free Speech*. Wells knew that it would not be safe for her to return to Tennessee, so she went to England to gain international support for her crusade against lynching.

She returned to the United States, and in 1895 she married attorney Ferdinand Lee Barnett, who owned and edited a weekly black newspaper. That same year she published the *Red Record*, which recorded the results of her investigation into the practice of lynching in America. In most of the seven hundred cases Wells documented in the report, the victim was accused of sexually attacking a white woman. The study revealed these accusations to be false and a smoke screen for underlying racial hatred.

For the rest of her life, Wells continued to make the public aware about the prevalence of lynching and was one of the few voices to openly challenge the practice. In 1909, she helped found the National Association for the Advancement of Colored People (NAACP). She died in 1931.

After white residents of Memphis, Tennessee, killed one of her friends, journalist Ida B. Wells began an antilynching crusade in the United States and in England.

MOSS. ENG. CO.
N.Y.

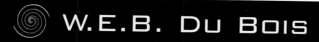

W.E.B. Du Bois

PROFESSOR AND AUTHOR FOUGHT FOR RACIAL EQUALITY

William Edward Burghardt (W.E.B.) Du Bois was born in 1868 in Massachusetts. A bright student, Du Bois studied with some of the most important social thinkers of his time. In 1896, he became the first black man to receive a doctorate in philosophy from Harvard University.

Du Bois worked as a professor, and in 1903 his work *The Souls of Black Folk*, a collection of essays in which he defined some of the key themes of the black experience, was published. Du Bois felt that the way to achieve racial equality was through what he termed "ceaseless agitation and insistent demand," and he urged African American people to use every resource they could to reach their goals.

In his papers, Du Bois criticized Booker T. Washington, another African American educator of the time, for not teaching enough basic academics to students. He felt that Washington focused too much on teaching menial working skills to blacks, when they needed to learn about art, literature, science, and math. It was through these core subjects that Du Bois felt blacks could achieve equality. Du Bois's views provided a new area of focus for the budding civil rights movement.

In 1905, Du Bois helped found the

W.E.B. Du Bois (opposite) was a founder of the National Association for the Advancement of Colored People and spent many hours in the offices of Crisis (above) as editor of the organization's journal.

Niagara Movement, a group of black leaders who fought for racial equality. He also helped to form the National Association for the Advancement of Colored People (NAACP), which adopted many of the goals of the Niagara Movement, and for more than twenty-four years he was director and editor of the organization's journal, *Crisis*.

As Du Bois aged, his opinions began to change. He began to support Pan-Africanism, which essentially believed that blacks should return to Africa because they would never achieve equality in America. He also began to support the concept of socialism (a system in which the government controls the economy and goods are owned collectively). In 1963, frustrated with the slow progress toward racial equality in the United State, Du Bois exiled himself to Ghana. He died there soon after at the age of ninety-five.

JAMES FARMER

FOUNDED THE CONGRESS OF RACIAL EQUALITY

James Farmer was born in Marshall, Texas, in 1920, the son of a preacher and professor of philosophy and religion. He received a degree from Wiley College and graduated from Howard University's School of Divinity, where he spent much of his time studying the nonviolent teachings of Mohandas Gandhi, an Indian political leader and humanitarian.

Farmer worked with the Fellowship of Reconciliation (FOR), an organization that advocated nonviolence as a way to social change. While he was with FOR, Farmer began to plan a movement based on Gandhian principles of nonviolence and the use of tactics such as boycotts, pickets, and demonstrations to achieve its goals. In 1942, Farmer helped to found the Congress of Racial Equality (CORE) to fight racism and challenge segregation, but it was not until the 1950s that CORE became very active.

Farmer and CORE were on the front lines of protests such as the Montgomery bus boycott and sit-ins, where they were asked to provide guidance and training on the techniques of nonviolent protest. When Farmer was appointed as CORE'S national director in 1961, he immediately began to organize Freedom Rides to challenge Supreme Court rulings that prohibited segregation on interstate travel. Farmer and CORE members were often met with hostility and brutality from citizens unwilling to accept the new laws, but they caught the attention of the news media and forced the government to take action. A commission banned segregated interstate transportation facilities, which committed the federal government to enforce the 1947 and 1960 Supreme Court rulings.

Farmer and CORE then became involved in the Mississippi Freedom Summer Project, which was designed to promote voter registration for African Americans. In 1964, three CORE members involved in the project were murdered. Shortly after, Farmer resigned from CORE and eventually ran for Congress. Although Farmer failed to win a seat, President Richard Nixon appointed him assistant secretary for administration of health, education, and welfare. In 1985, Farmer completed his autobiography, *Lay Bare the Heart*. In 1998, he was awarded the Presidential Medal of Freedom by President Bill Clinton. One year later, he died at the age of seventy-nine.

Influenced by the teachings of Indian leader Mohandas Gandhi, James Farmer organized the first chapter of Congress of Racial Equality and led the group in nonviolent protests.

Asa Philip Randolph was born in Florida in 1889. He was the son of a minister and graduated at the top of his class at Cookman Institute, the state's first high school for African Americans.

In his twenties, Randolph went to New York where he pursued an education in politics at City College. He later met Chandler Owen, a fellow student with whom he created a radical magazine called the *Messenger*. The publication's philosophy was that racism could be overcome if integration in the workplace was achieved, an unpopular message.

In 1925, Randolph was asked to lead the formation of the Brotherhood of Sleeping Car Porters (BSCP). Pullman train cars had beds on them, and porters were the people who attended to these cars. The company was the largest employer of African Americans in the nation. Randolph was the perfect choice as leader because he was an excellent speaker and not a porter, so he could not be fired. After he worked for more than a decade to organize the porters, Randolph succeeded in getting the Pullman Company to recognize the BSCP as the porters' official representative. The porters were given higher pay and fewer hours, a concession that Randolph called the "first victory of Negro workers over a great industrial corporation." Randolph believed that equality could only be achieved with economic opportunity and continued to fight for the rights of African American workers.

In 1940, Randolph called for ten thousand blacks to march in Washington, D.C., but when President Franklin D. Roosevelt issued an order that banned discrimination in defense industries, Randolph called off the march. When Randolph threatened the use of a similar technique of civil disobedience to fight the practice of segregation in the military, President Harry Truman issued an executive order that banned discrimination in the armed forces.

In 1963, Randolph again asked blacks to march on Washington. His plans resulted in the largest civil rights demonstration ever held in the United States. While the credit for this event is commonly given to the primary speaker, Martin Luther King Jr., it was Randolph who actually organized it. Randolph retired in 1968. Eleven years later he died at the age of ninety.

Asa Philip Randolph helped found the Brotherhood of Sleeping Car Porters and also organized two major marches on Washington to promote fair employment for African Americans.

THURGOOD MARSHALL

FIRST AFRICAN AMERICAN ON THE SUPREME COURT

Thurgood Marshall was born in 1908 in Maryland, the grandson of a slave. His father taught him an appreciation of the Constitution and the importance of law. After high school he attended Lincoln University in Pennsylvania.

Later, Marshall studied at Howard University, a small all-black law school. He then entered private practice and served as legal counsel for the National Association for the Advancement of Colored People (NAACP) for almost thirty years. Known to many as "Mr. Civil Rights," Marshall represented a wide variety of clients in cases that involved racial justice. He participated in campaigns to force white storeowners to hire black salespeople and to get Maryland congressmen to support an antilynching bill, and he prepared cases against the University of Mississippi and the University of Texas on behalf of black students.

Marshall helped blacks achieve justice through the interpretation of the law. He argued thirty-two cases before the Supreme Court and was victorious in twenty-nine of them. In 1944, in *Smith v. Allwright*, he won a victory for black voting rights when he successfully argued against the exclusion of African American voters in primary elections. Four years later, in *Shelley v. Kraemer*, he argued that it was illegal to refuse to sell a home to an African American. The case that

Opposite: Thurgood Marshall used his extensive knowledge of the law to fight for civil rights. Above: Appointed in 1967 by President Lyndon Johnson (left), Marshall (right) became the first African American to serve on the U.S. Supreme Court.

propelled Marshall into the headlines, however, came along in 1954. In *Brown v. Board of Education of Topeka, Kansas*, Marshall argued against segregation in all public schools and won.

In 1962 Marshall was appointed as judge to the Second U.S. Circuit Court of Appeals. In 1965 he was given the post of U.S. solicitor general. Two years later he became the first African American nominated to the Supreme Court, where he voted to uphold every gender and racial affirmative action policy challenged. Marshall retired in 1991 and died in 1993.

ADAM CLAYTON POWELL JR.

PROMINENT AFRICAN AMERICAN CONGRESSMAN

Adam Clayton Powell Jr. was born in 1908 in New Haven. Connecticut, the son of Reverend Clayton Powell, a successful Harlem preacher. He grew up in New York City and received degrees from Colgate and Columbia Universities.

At the age of twenty-nine, he took over his father's Harlem church. An impressive speaker, he attracted thousands of people to the church and campaigned for issues such as better housing and more jobs for African Americans. Powell headed a relief program that handed out food and clothing to the needy in his community and formed the Greater New York Coordinating Committee on Employment, a group that used pickets and boycotts against businesses that discriminated against blacks.

In 1941, Powell was the first African American elected to the New York City Council. Three years later, he became the first African American elected to Congress from the northeast. He went on to serve eleven terms in Congress (1945–1971). During his years there, he refused to be treated any differently than his white colleagues and often took his black constituents to whites-only eating establishments. Powell would attach to proposed federal funding bills a provision, known as the Powell amendment, which called for no federal money to be allocated to an agency or district that practiced discrimination. Years later, the Powell amendment was enacted into law as Title VI of the landmark Civil Rights Act of 1964. Powell also established his own newspaper, the *People's Voice*, through which he crusaded for jobs and the poor.

In 1961, Powell became chairman of the Committee on Education and Labor, the first African American congressman to head such an important committee. His effective leadership in this position was marred by negative publicity about a 1958 tax evasion charge.

Despite Powell's many achievements, some people did not appreciate his working style. On January 9, 1967, Powell was expelled from Congress and stripped of his chairmanship because of accusations of mismanaging the committee's budget, numerous trips taken at public expense, and absenteeism. Two years later the U.S. Supreme Court declared his expulsion unconstitutional.

Powell was the first prominent African American voice in Congress, and his persistent calls for justice fueled the civil rights movement at a time when African Americans had few representatives in government. His autobiography, *Adam by Adam*, was published in 1971. Powell died in Miami, Florida, in 1972.

Adam Clayton Powell Jr. was the first black member elected to the New York City Council.

Rosa McCauley was born in Tuskegee, Alabama, in 1913. After being home-schooled until she was eleven, Rosa attended a private school. Later, she went on to Alabama State College. In 1932, she married a man named Raymond Parks.

In 1955, after a long day at work, Parks boarded her usual bus in Montgomery, Alabama, and sat down in a seat toward the middle, where either whites or blacks could sit. When the bus became crowded, the bus driver told Parks to give up her seat for a white man standing in the aisle, but she refused. Parks was arrested, jailed, and found guilty of violating a segregation law. The head of the local chapter of the National Association for the Advancement of Colored People (NAACP), E.D. Nixon, vowed to appeal her conviction. Nixon knew that Parks was the right person to help the NAACP push through new bus desegregation laws.

The NAACP and Parks organized a citywide boycott of the bus system. African Americans throughout the area refused to ride, and the bus lines felt the financial loss because three-fourths of their customers were black. The boycott was meant to last for one day; however, it lasted for almost an entire year and cost the bus company more than $750,000. Since Nixon traveled frequently, another person was put in charge of the boycott—a young preacher named Martin Luther King Jr. Meanwhile, Parks's supporters continued her legal appeals. A year after Parks refused to give up her bus seat, the Supreme Court declared segregation on public transportation illegal.

Opposite: Rosa Parks proved that every individual has the power to enact change. Above: When police arrested Parks for refusing to give her seat on a bus to a white man, Parks and the NAACP organized a boycott that sparked the civil rights movement.

The actions of Rosa Parks inspired the belief in the power of the individual to enact change and earned her the title of the "Mother of the Civil Rights Movement." Parks moved to Detroit in 1957. She worked as a secretary and office assistant for Congressman John Conyers until she retired in 1988. In 1996, Parks received the Presidential Medal of Freedom.

FANNIE LOU TOWNSEND HAMER

FOUGHT FOR PASSAGE OF THE VOTING RIGHTS ACT

Fannie Lou Townsend was born in 1917 in Mississippi. She was the youngest of twenty children of sharecroppers and worked hard in the cotton fields most of her life. In 1945, she married Perry Hamer, with whom she worked on a white man's plantation.

In the early 1960s, Hamer attended a Student Nonviolent Coordinating Committee (SNCC) meeting where she became inspired to exercise her right to vote. At the time, the threat of violence and strict literacy requirements made voting almost impossible for African Americans. When Hamer and others could not interpret the Mississippi constitution to the satisfaction of the white registrars, they were turned away. Later, she was fired from her job at the plantation for her attempts to vote.

In the fall of 1962, Hamer began to work for the SNCC. A year later, as she returned from a voter education training session, Hamer and a few other civil rights workers were arrested for entering a whites-only restaurant to eat, and taken to jail. She, like others, was beaten severely by several other black prisoners who were ordered to do so by the police.

Undaunted, Hamer continued to work with the SNCC. Although uneducated, she was a powerful speaker who was often referred to as the female equivalent of the compelling preacher Martin Luther King Jr. She cofounded the Mississippi Freedom Democratic Party (MFDP) to give blacks in Mississippi an alternative to the traditional Democratic Party, which excluded them. Hamer spoke out against the unwillingness of the Democratic Party to seat MFDP delegates at the Democratic National Convention in 1964, even though the MFDP got more votes than the Democrats in the Mississippi primary. Her speech motivated many people throughout the nation to fight against racial discrimination, and in years to come, MFDP candidates were elected to local and state offices.

The work of Hamer and the MFDP was also partly responsible for the passage of the Voting Rights Act of 1965, which made it illegal to deny any adult citizen the right to vote and guaranteed federal enforcement of that right. In her last ten years, Hamer focused on low-income housing, child care, and school desegregation. She died in 1977 at the age of sixty. Her headstone is engraved with her famous line: "I'm sick and tired of being sick and tired."

Fannie Lou Townsend Hamer was a powerful speaker who became one of the most recognized women in the civil rights movement.

George Wallace was born on a farm in 1919 in Alabama. He became a Golden Gloves champion while in high school and later worked his way through law school by boxing professionally.

After he graduated from the law program at the University of Alabama in 1942, Wallace spent a brief time in the air force and then went to work as assistant attorney general for Alabama. In 1947, he was elected to the state legislature. During most of the 1950s, he worked as a judge in the Third Judicial Circuit Court. In 1958, he campaigned for governor of Alabama with the endorsement of the NAACP and spoke out against the Ku Klux Klan, a racist organization that believed in white supremacy. When Wallace lost to his opponent, a segregationist, he decided to change his position on racial equality.

Wallace ran for governor again in 1962, and this time he won. In his inaugural speech in 1963, he promised "Segregation now! Segregation tomorrow! Segregation forever!" He lived up to that promise and opposed each and every attempt by the government to end segregation—especially in schools.

On June 10, 1963, a federal judge ordered the University of Alabama to open its doors to two black students. As the new governor, Wallace blocked the entrance. When President John F. Kennedy placed the Alabama National Guard under federal authority, however, Wallace stepped aside.

In September, Kennedy again intervened when Wallace ordered state troopers and National Guardsmen to prevent Birmingham schools from being integrated. Wallace's defense of segregation made him enormously popular among voters who opposed integration, and he became a leading spokesman for resistance to change.

The governor ran for president in 1964 and 1968 and lost both times. He tried once more, but during the campaign, a man named Arthur Bremer shot him. The shot paralyzed him below the waist and ended his presidential aspirations. Nevertheless, Wallace returned to serve as governor for three more terms. By the end of Wallace's last term in 1986, his attitude had changed. He publicly apologized for the role he had played in opposition to civil rights and asked for forgiveness. Wallace died at the age of seventy-nine.

As governor of Alabama, George Wallace attempted to block every federal attempt to desegregate schools. Wallace publicly apologized for his actions more than twenty years later.

GEORGE C. WALLAC
GOVERNOR

Born in Atlanta, Georgia, in 1929, Martin Luther King Jr. was the son of a Georgia minister. In 1948, he was ordained and made assistant pastor in his father's church. He earned a bachelor's degree in Divinity and later attended Boston University where he earned a doctorate. Influenced by the teachings of Mohandas Gandhi, King believed that nonviolence was the best way to achieve civil rights reform.

King was asked to handle a bus boycott in Montgomery, Alabama, prompted by the arrest of a black woman, Rosa Parks, for her refusal to give up her seat on a Montgomery bus. His expert handling of the boycott allowed King to emerge as a national leader of the civil rights movement.

In August 1957, King and other black ministers founded the Southern Christian Leadership Conference (SCLC) to build upon the success at Montgomery. After a trip to West Africa and India, he moved his family to Atlanta to devote his efforts to the SCLC. At the beginning of the sit-in movement, King helped students form the Student Nonviolent Coordinating Committee (SNCC).

King organized a series of mass demonstrations throughout the South in support of a new civil rights bill. In one such demonstration in Birmingham, Alabama, a group of marchers were attacked by fire hoses and police dogs, and King was arrested and jailed. While imprisoned he wrote "Letter from Birmingham Jail," one of the most famous commentaries on the civil rights movement. When the public viewed on television the violence the demonstrators were subjected to, national opinion swayed in favor of King and his cause.

In 1963, King again captured the attention of the entire country with an inspirational speech called "I Have a Dream," which he delivered on the steps of the Lincoln Memorial at a march in Washington, D.C. The speech was intended to garner support for a comprehensive civil rights act that was then in Congress.

Violence again erupted in 1965, in Selma, Alabama, when King launched a drive in support of a federal voting rights law for African Americans. State troopers beat black marchers, and a young black deacon and a white minister were killed. Again, the public was horrified, and when King asked for help, thousands came from all over the nation to Selma. Congress responded by passing the 1965 Voting Rights Act, which made it illegal to hinder the voting process and empowered the U.S. attorney

From his leadership role in the Montgomery bus boycott in 1955 to his assassination in 1968, Martin Luther King Jr. devoted his life to achieving racial equality through nonviolence.

general to supervise elections in southern states where blacks were traditionally kept from the polls.

King's philosophies of nonviolent protest and his dedication to the civil rights movement provided leadership and direction to years of civil rights activities that prompted important legislation and instilled African Americans with a sense of worth. In 1964, the thirty-five-year-old King received the Nobel Peace Prize and became the youngest recipient of the award. In 1968, King went to Memphis to support a group of striking sanitation workers. As he stood on the balcony of his hotel room, he was shot and killed by assassin James Earl Ray. When the news was announced, riots broke out in more than one hundred cities. It was a dark moment for the movement and for the nation. In 1986, King's birthday, January 15, became a national holiday.

King speaks to a crowd of marchers that gathered in Selma, Alabama, in response to his call for support of federal voting rights for African Americans. As a result, Congress passed the 1965 Voting Rights Act.

Malcolm X was born Malcolm Little in 1925 in Omaha, Nebraska, one of eight children. The family later moved to Lansing, Michigan. In 1929, white racists burned down the Littles' home, and two years later, Malcolm's father died. When the state welfare agency placed Malcolm and his siblings in state institutions and boarding homes, his mother had an emotional breakdown and was confined in a mental hospital.

In his teens, Little moved to the northeast. In 1946, he was arrested in Boston for burglary and sentenced to ten years in prison. While he was in jail, he discovered a form of Islamic religion known as the Nation of Islam (also called the Black Muslims). The Nation of Islam, led by Elijah Muhammad, believed blacks were created first by God, or Allah, and that whites were evil.

The Black Muslim belief that last names were the names of white slaveholders led Little to change his name to Malcolm X upon his release from prison in 1952. He became an Islamic minister and worked closely with Muhammad. Malcolm's skills as a speaker and recruiter and organizer of temples became evident. He used the news media to share the tenets of Islam and brought membership from a few hundred to more than thirty thousand.

Malcolm X's beliefs offered an alternative to the integration and nonviolence taught by other civil rights leaders such as Martin Luther King Jr. Malcolm X preached that nonviolent confrontations, racial equality, and integration were ridiculous. He believed the solution to be a return to Africa or the division of the United States into black and white nations.

Eventually, tensions arose between Malcolm and Muhammad. In March 1964, Malcolm X announced that he was leaving the Nation of Islam. In April he left for the Islamic holy city of Mecca, Saudi Arabia, and then traveled throughout Africa and the Middle East. There, he adopted the name el-Hajj Malik el-Shabazz and reversed his earlier position that whites were inherently racist.

In June 1964, Malcolm formed the Organization of Afro-American Unity to unify blacks with differing philosophies and to work with forward-thinking white organizations. He also worked to bring the issue of American racism to the United Nations. In February 1965, his home was firebombed, but his family escaped unharmed. A week later, the thirty-nine-year-old Malcolm was shot and killed by a Black Muslim at a rally of his followers in Harlem.

A charismatic speaker and member of the Nation of Islam, Malcolm X advocated that blacks either return to Africa or live in a blacks-only nation within a divided United States.

JESSE JACKSON

FOUNDED OPERATION PUSH

J esse Jackson was born in 1941 in South Carolina. After high school, he left the South to attend the University of Illinois on an athletic scholarship. Eventually he chose to transfer to the North Carolina Agricultural and Technical College (A&T), where he earned his degree. While there he joined the Greensboro chapter of the Congress on Racial Equality (CORE) and participated in and organized sit-ins and marches in an attempt to desegregate public places, such as restaurants. His efforts earned him much recognition regionally.

After graduation from North Carolina A&T, Jackson attended the Chicago Theological Seminary, but left before finishing his coursework to focus all his efforts on the civil rights movement. In 1965, he aligned himself with Martin Luther King Jr., and joined the Southern Christian Leadership Conference (SCLC). The next year he began work on the SCLC program Operation Breadbasket, which organized Chicago's black community to selectively buy from black manufacturers and retailers. Operation Breadbasket also placed pressure on white-owned businesses to buy products made by blacks and to hire black employees. One year later, Jackson became the program's national director.

In 1971, Jackson resigned from the SCLC and established Operation PUSH (People United to Serve Humanity) to improve the overall economic status of African Americans. Jackson worked to protect black homeowners, workers, and businesses. In keeping with his belief that the primary key to achieving these goals was through political power, he traveled for months to urge black people to register to vote. Jackson soon became a visible and in-demand speaker on the topic of civil rights. His strong media presence and oratorical skills helped win support for the civil rights movement.

In 1984, Jackson unsuccessfully ran for the Democratic Party's nomination for president. Four years later, a wiser, more prepared Jackson ran again and finished second to Michael Dukakis. Since that time, Jackson has focused on foreign affairs. In 2000, President Bill Clinton awarded Jackson with the Presidential Medal of Freedom. Jackson's son, Jesse Jackson Jr., became a congressman in 1995.

Jesse Jackson founded Operation PUSH in 1971 to improve the economic status of African American workers, businesses, and homeowners.

1862	Abraham Lincoln's Emancipation Proclamation frees Southern slaves.
1865	Thirteenth Amendment abolishes slavery.
1868	Fourteenth Amendment guarantees black Americans citizenship and equal protection of the laws.
1870	Fifteenth Amendment bans race discrimination in voting.
1875	Civil Rights Act of 1875 bans race discrimination in public places and on juries.
1882–1901	Lynchings become epidemic in South.
1883	Supreme Court ruling invalidates part of the 1875 act.
1896	Doctrine in *Plessy v. Ferguson* defines "separate but equal" race relations in America.
1909	National Association for the Advancement of Colored People (NAACP) is formed.
1954	*Brown v. Board of Education of Topeka, Kansas* demands school integration, which overturns *Plessy v. Ferguson*.
1955	Rosa Parks arrested in Montgomery, Alabama, which sparks the Montgomery Bus Boycott; Martin Luther King Jr. emerges as leader for the civil rights movement.
1956	Supreme Court rules that segregated seating on Montgomery buses is unconstitutional.
1960	Students stage sit-in at an all-white lunch counter at a Woolworth's department store in Greensboro, North Carolina.

In 1961, black and white activists protested segregation by riding together in buses through the South. These Freedom Riders faced violence, including the burning of their buses.

1963	250,000 demonstrators march on Washington, D.C.; Alabama governor George Wallace tries to stop attempts to prevent desegregation of the University of Alabama; President John F. Kennedy is assassinated.
1964	The Civil Rights Act of 1964 bans racial discrimination in public places.
1965	Congress passes the Voting Rights Act of 1965; Malcolm X is assassinated.
1968	Martin Luther King Jr. is assassinated.
1986	Martin Luther King Jr. Day is established.

FOR FURTHER INFORMATION

BOOKS

Jules Archer, *They Had a Dream: The Civil Rights' Struggle from Frederick Douglass to Marcus Garvey to Martin Luther King to Malcolm X.* New York: Puffin, 1996.

Casey King and Linda Barrett Osborne, *Oh Freedom! Kids Talk About the Civil Rights Movement with the People Who Made It Happen.* New York: Knopf, 1997.

Ellen Levine, *Freedom's Child: Young Civil Rights Activists Tell Their Own Stories.* New York: Puffin, 2000.

Rosa Parks, *Dear Mrs. Parks: A Dialogue with Today's Youth.* New York: Lee and Low, 1997.

Richard Wormser, *The Rise and Fall of Jim Crow.* New York: St. Martin's, 2003.

WEBSITES

We Shall Overcome
www.cr.nps.gov
A web site presented by the National Register of Historic Places that features links to important sites and events.

InfoPlease
www.infoplease.com
A site that presents a detailed time line of events, each one linking the visitor to further information.

Greensboro Sit-Ins
www.sitins.com
A detailed look at the national sit-ins by Dr. George Farmer.

ABOUT THE AUTHOR

Tamra B. Orr is a full-time freelance writer and author. She has written more than two dozen nonfiction books for children and families, including *Fire Ants, The Journey of Lewis and Clark, The Biography of Astronaut Alan Shepard,* and *The Parent's Guide to Homeschooling.* Orr attended Ball State University and received a bachelor's degree in secondary education and English in 1982. Orr lives in Portland, Oregon, with her husband and four children, who range in age from seven to seventeen. She enjoys her job as an author because it teaches her something new every day.

INDEX